TROLL
TREASURY OF
CHRISTMAS

TROLL
TREASURY OF
CHRISTMAS

Edited by John C. Miles
Illustrated by Elizabeth De Lisle,
Wendy Purdy, and Graham Dennison

Troll Associates

Library of Congress Cataloging-in-Publication Data

Treasury of Christmas / edited by John C. Miles; illustrated by
  Elizabeth De Lisle, Wendy Purdy, and Graham Dennison.
      p.   cm.
    Summary: Poems, Bible stories, fiction, carols, informational
  articles, customs, lore, and handicraft relating to Christmas.
    ISBN 0-8167-2236-6 (lib. bdg.)   ISBN 0-8167-2237-4 (pbk.)
    1. Christmas—Literary collections.   [1. Christmas—Literary
  collections.   2. Christmas decorations.]   I. Miles, John C., 1960-
  . II. De Lisle, Elizabeth, ill.   III. Purdy, Wendy, ill.
  IV. Dennison, Graham, ill.
  PZ5.T748 1991
  808.8 '033—dc20   90-39372

Published in the U.S.A. by Troll Associates, Inc.,
100 Corporate Drive, Mahwah, New Jersey.
Produced for Troll Associates, Inc., by
Joshua Morris Publishing Inc. in association
with Harper Collins.
Copyright © 1991 by Harper Collins.
All rights reserved.
Printed in Belgium.
10 9 8 7 6 5 4 3 2 1

CONTENTS

The Night Before Christmas
by Clement C. Moore

'Twas the night before Christmas, when all through the house,
Not a creature was stirring, not even a mouse.
The stockings were hung by the chimney with care,
In hopes that St. Nicholas soon would be there.
The children were nestled all snug in their beds,
While visions of sugarplums danced in their heads;
And Mama in her kerchief, and I in my cap,
Had just settled our brains for a long winter's nap,
When out on the lawn there arose such a clatter,
I sprang from my bed to see what was the matter.

Away to the window I flew like a flash,
Tore open the shutters and threw up the sash.
The moon on the breast of the new-fallen snow
Gave the luster of midday to objects below;
When what to my wondering eyes should appear,
But a miniature sleigh and eight tiny reindeer,
With a little old driver, so lively and quick,
I knew in a moment it must be St. Nick!

More rapid than eagles his coursers they came,
And he whistled and shouted and called them by name:
"Now, Dasher! now, Dancer! now, Prancer and Vixen!
On, Comet! on, Cupid! on, Donder and Blitzen!
To the top of the porch! to the top of the wall!
Now dash away! dash away! dash away, all!"

As dry leaves that before the wild hurricane fly,
When they meet with an obstacle, mount to the sky,
So up to the housetop the coursers they flew,
With the sleigh full of toys, and St. Nicholas, too.
And then in a twinkling I heard on the roof
The prancing and pawing of each little hoof.
As I drew in my head and was turning around,
Down the chimney St. Nicholas came with a bound.

He was dressed all in fur, from his head to his foot,
And his clothes were all tarnished with ashes and soot;
A bundle of toys he had flung on his back,
And he looked like a peddler just opening his pack.
His eyes how they twinkled! his dimples how merry!
His cheeks were like roses, his nose like a cherry!
His droll little mouth was drawn up like a bow,
And the beard on his chin was as white as the snow.

The stump of a pipe he held tight in his teeth,
And the smoke it encircled his head like a wreath.
He had a broad face and a little round belly
That shook, when he laughed, like a bowl full of jelly.
He was chubby and plump, a right jolly old elf,
And I laughed when I saw him, in spite of myself.
A wink of his eye and a twist of his head
Soon gave me to know I had nothing to dread.
He spoke not a word, but went straight to his work,
And filled all the stockings, then turned with a jerk,
And laying his finger aside of his nose,
And giving a nod, up the chimney he rose.
He sprang to his sleigh, to his team gave a whistle,
And away they all flew like the down of a thistle.
But I heard him exclaim, ere he drove out of sight,
"Happy Christmas to all, and to all a good night!"

The Story of Christmas

Every year, people all over the world celebrate Christmas, the birthday of a little boy named Jesus. This is the story of his birth.

A long time ago, a young woman named Mary lived in the town of Nazareth in Galilee. She was engaged to marry a carpenter named Joseph. One day, when Mary was all alone, a brilliant light suddenly shone down on her from the sky. She was frightened, but a gentle voice said to her, "Do not be afraid, Mary, for you have found favor with God." It was the angel Gabriel, sent by God. "Behold, you will bear a son, and you shall call him Jesus. He will be the Savior of all the people." Then Gabriel and the light were gone.

Months later, when Mary's baby was almost due, the Roman emperor ordered all the people in the land to go back to the place where they were born. He wanted to count them, so he could know exactly how many people lived in his land.

Joseph came from Bethlehem, so he and Mary went there together. But when they reached the city, they found it crowded with people. There was no place for them to stay. Finally, an innkeeper told them they could sleep in his stable.

Jesus was born that night in the stable. Mary wrapped him in swaddling clothes and laid him in a manger.

That same night, some shepherds were tending their sheep nearby when an angel of God appeared. "Don't be afraid," said the angel, "for I bring you tidings of great joy. Tonight your Savior was born. Go to Bethlehem, where you will find the baby lying in a manger."

Suddenly, the air was filled with a chorus of angels singing:

"Glory to God in the highest,
and peace to his people on earth."

When the angels had gone, the shepherds hurried to Bethlehem. They found Mary, Joseph, and the baby in the stable. The shepherds knelt down and worshiped Jesus, for they knew that the angel's words were true.

When they left the stable, the shepherds ran through the town. They told everyone of the wonders they had seen.

A Christmas Carol

Adapted from the story by Charles Dickens

CHAPTER ONE - THE MISER

There was never a stingier, greedier old miser than Ebenezer Scrooge. He had never been known to give away a penny in his life or to say a kind word to anybody. Even on a warm day, he seemed frozen to the bone. No one ever stopped him in the street to say, "Hello there, Ebenezer! Nice to see you!" The cold, heartless look on his face made everyone avoid him. But old Scrooge did not mind much. In fact, he preferred things that way. He had no time for people who went around laughing and enjoying themselves. As far as he was concerned, they were all fools.

One Christmas Eve, Scrooge sat as usual at his office desk. Passing by the office windows were people shivering and stamping their feet to keep warm. Even though the clocks in the city had just struck three o'clock, it was already dark. Candles were lit in the nearby windows. A thick cloud of fog hung over everything, hiding the houses across the street.

Scrooge kept the door of his office open so that he could keep his eye on Bob Cratchit, his employee. Cratchit sat in a dark, dismal room across the hall. Scrooge had a small fire in his office, but Bob Cratchit's fire was even smaller. Yet he was afraid to add more coal. Why? Because Scrooge kept the extra coal in his office. And every time Bob crossed the hall for more, Scrooge threatened to dismiss him. Bob Cratchit was very poor and had a family to support. So rather than lose his job, he just put on his scarf and tried to warm his hands over his candle.

"Merry Christmas, Uncle! God bless you!" cried a bright voice. It was the voice of Scrooge's nephew, Fred, who had burst in so quickly that he made Scrooge jump.

"Bah! Humbug!" said Scrooge.

Fred was glowing with health after his brisk walk in the cold air. His cheeks were red and his eyes sparkled. "Christmas is not a humbug, Uncle!" he cried. "Come on, you don't mean that!"

"I do," said Scrooge. "Merry Christmas indeed! What right have you got to be so merry? You're poor enough."

"Well," said Fred merrily, "you're rich enough. What right have you got to be so grumpy?"

Scrooge could not come up with a better answer and could only say "Bah!" again and then "Humbug!"

"Don't get angry, Uncle," pleaded his nephew.

"How else should I feel?" said Scrooge. "Away with Christmas! It's only a time for paying bills and finding yourself a year older but not a penny richer. If I had my way, every idiot who goes around shouting 'Merry Christmas' would be boiled in his own Christmas gravy."

"Uncle!" protested Fred.

"Nephew!" said Scrooge sternly. "You celebrate Christmas in your way, and I'll celebrate it in mine!"

"Celebrate it?" repeated the young man. "But you don't celebrate it."

"Let me ignore it then," said Scrooge. "A whole lot of good it has ever done you."

"Christmas has always been good to me," said Fred. "I always think of it as the best time of year. It's the only time in the whole year when men and women open their hearts and think of people for a change. So Uncle, even though it has never made me a penny richer, it has done me good and it will do me good. Long live Christmas, I say!"

Bob Cratchit overheard this in his little office and could not help clapping his hands at the end of this speech.

"One more peep out of you, Cratchit," warned Scrooge, "and you can celebrate Christmas by losing your job!"

"Don't be angry, Uncle," said Fred. "Come and have supper with us tomorrow."

"I'd be out of my mind if I did," said Scrooge.

"But why?" asked his nephew.

"Why were you silly enough to get married?" asked Scrooge, who did not approve of anyone as poor as his nephew having a wife.

"Because I fell in love."

"Bah!" grunted Scrooge, who seemed to think that was even sillier than celebrating Christmas. "Good-bye!"

"But Uncle, you never came to see me before I was married. Why make that an excuse for not coming now?"

"Good-bye!" said Scrooge.

"I have tried to make friends with you because of Christmas, and I'm not going to let you spoil my day," said Fred. "So a merry Christmas to you, Uncle."

"Good-bye!" said Scrooge.

"And a happy new year!"

Fred left the room without having said a single unkind word. He stopped in the outer office to say "Merry Christmas!" to Bob Cratchit. Bob's response was warmer than Scrooge's, and he returned the greetings with all his might.

Scrooge overheard him and muttered, "There's another idiot talking about a merry Christmas."

After Scrooge's nephew had left, two men came in.

"The offices of Scrooge and Marley, I believe," said one of the men. "Are you Mr. Scrooge or Mr. Marley?"

"Mr. Marley has been dead for seven years," replied Scrooge. "He died on Christmas Eve seven years ago."

"Well, Mr. Scrooge," said the other man, "at this festive time of the year we must do what we can to help the poor."

"Are there no prisons?" asked Scrooge.

"Plenty of prisons."

"What about the workhouses?"

"Plenty of workhouses," replied the man. "We are trying to raise money to buy food and warm clothing for the poor. What shall I put you down for?"

"Nothing," replied Scrooge. "I can't afford to make lazy people merry.

They can go to the workhouse."

"Many would rather die than enter a workhouse."

"Let them die then," said Scrooge. "Good day, gentlemen."

The two men went off empty-handed, and once more Scrooge buried himself in his work.

Meanwhile, the fog and darkness thickened outside. The cold became more bitter. Some workmen had lit a huge fire. A group of ragged men and boys huddled all around the blaze, trying to warm their frozen bodies.

Just then, a cold, ragged little boy stooped down at Scrooge's keyhole and began to sing a Christmas carol. But he got no farther than "God rest you, merry gentlemen! Let nothing you dismay!" before Scrooge angrily

shook his ruler at him. The singer ran away in terror.

Finally, it was time for closing up the office.

"I suppose you'll want a holiday tomorrow?" Scrooge said to Bob Cratchit.

"If it is quite convenient, sir."

"It's not convenient," said Scrooge.

"It's only once a year, sir," said Bob.

"A poor excuse," grumbled Scrooge, buttoning up his overcoat. "But I suppose you must have the whole day. Just be here earlier the next morning to make up for it." And Scrooge walked out with a growl.

Bob Cratchit closed up the office. Then he wrapped his scarf tighter around his neck – he could not afford a winter coat – and hurried home as fast as he could.

CHAPTER TWO · MARLEY'S GHOST

Scrooge lived in the house that belonged to his dead partner, Jacob Marley. It was a dreary place, and Scrooge had to feel his way through the unlit front yard to reach the door. There was a large brass knocker on it.

As he put his key in the door's keyhole, Scrooge glanced up. There in the knocker, instead of a lion's head, he saw Marley's face! It was a ghostly face. How could it be anything else when Marley had been dead for seven years? Scrooge gasped and jumped back. Then the face vanished.

Scrooge hurried inside and lit his candle. He paused and looked behind him, as if he almost expected to see Marley's ghost following him into the hall. But there was nothing to be seen, so he said, "Bah! Humbug!" to reassure himself.

Still carrying his candle, Scrooge went through each of his dingy rooms to see that all was in order. There was a small fire in the living room with a little pot of broth hanging over it. There was also a spoon and bowl lying ready.

Satisfied that all was well, Scrooge shut the door and locked himself in. Then he took off his coat, put on his robe, his slippers, and his nightcap, and sat down in front of the fire to eat his broth.

It was a very small fire, and Scrooge had to sit very close to it before he could feel any warmth at all. There were pictures on the cracked tiles

around the old fireplace. As Scrooge stared at them, he seemed to see the face of his dead partner, Jacob Marley, once more.

"Humbug!" said Scrooge. Then he leaned his head back in his chair. His glance happened to fall on an old, unused bell that hung in the room. The bell had begun to swing. At first, it scarcely made a sound. But soon it rang out with a loud clang, which was answered by all the other bells in the house.

Suddenly, all bells stopped. Then came a clanking sound from down below, as if someone was dragging a heavy chain up the stairs.

"It's still humbug," muttered Scrooge to himself. "I won't believe it."

No sooner had he spoken than something came straight through the door. It was a ghost! There was no doubt about who it was, either. It had Marley's face, coat, hat, and boots. The chain that clanked around his feet was made of cash registers, keys, padlocks, bankbooks, deeds, and heavy bags of money. His body was transparent. So Scrooge could look right through him and see the cracks in the wall behind him.

Scrooge still could not believe his eyes. "What do you want?" he demanded.

"Much." There was no doubt that it was Marley's voice.

"Can you sit down?" asked Scrooge, looking doubtfully at him.

"I can."

"Do it then."

The ghost sat down at the other side of the fireplace. "You don't believe in me," he said, looking at Scrooge.

"I don't," said Scrooge. "It's only humbug. Humbug, I tell you!"

Suddenly, the ghost gave a mournful wail and shook his chains with a terrible noise.

"Mercy!" Scrooge cried. "Why have you come here to trouble me? And why are you wearing all those chains?"

"I am wearing the chains I made during my lifetime," said the ghost. "I am doomed to wander over the face of the earth and to carry them with me wherever I go."

Every bone in Scrooge's body was trembling by now.

"I have no choice," said the ghost. "I cannot rest. I cannot pause anywhere. I must travel on many weary journeys."

"But you have been dead for seven years," said Scrooge. "Have you been traveling all that time?"

"All that time. No rest, no peace. Only the terrible torture of guilt and remorse."

"But you were always a good man of business, Jacob."

"Business! I ought to have made mankind my business, not money. When did I ever give money to charity or show anyone any kindness while I was on earth?" asked the ghost. "I am here tonight to warn you, Ebenezer

Scrooge, that you still have a chance of escaping my fate."

"Thank you," said Scrooge, white with fear.

"You will be haunted by three ghosts. Expect the first when the clock strikes one. Expect the second on the next night at the same time. The third will come when the last stroke of twelve has ceased to ring on the next night. Mark my words, and remember them for your own sake."

The ghost stood up and moved backward toward the window. Then he floated out into the dark night.

Scrooge walked over and looked out the window. The air was full of phantoms that moaned as they moved and wearily clanked their heavy chains. Scrooge had known many of them when they were alive. Some were chained with heavy iron safes, and they all looked miserable.

Scrooge wanted to say "Humbug!" But he was still so weak with fear that he could not even speak. Then, feeling quite tired, he stretched out on his bed and soon fell asleep.

CHAPTER THREE

THE FIRST OF THE THREE SPIRITS

It was very dark when Scrooge woke up. The church bell had begun to strike. Twelve! Surely the clock was wrong. It had been after two o'clock when he went to bed. How could it be twelve now? "Can I have slept through a whole day and into another night?" Scrooge said to himself.

He thought about Marley's ghost again. Surely it had all been a dream . . . hadn't it? Suddenly, he remembered that Marley had said he would be haunted by the first ghost as the bell tolled one. He listened to the bells as they rang out every fifteen minutes. And on the stroke of one, a strange light flashed into the room. The drapes around his bed pulled apart.

Scrooge sat up in an instant and found himself face to face with his ghostly visitor. He was a strange figure — in some ways, like a child; in others, like an old man. His hair was white, as if with age, and yet there was not a wrinkle on his face. The ghost wore a gown of pure white with a sparkling belt around his waist. A branch of fresh, green holly was in his hand.

"Are you the spirit who has come to haunt me?" asked Scrooge in a trembling voice.

"I am." The ghost spoke with a soft and gentle voice.

"Who are you?" asked Scrooge.

"I am the Ghost of Christmas Past."

"Long past?" asked Scrooge.

"I am the ghost of *your* past!" was the answer.

"What has brought you here?"

"I am here for your good. Get up and walk with me."

The spirit clasped him by the arm. Although his touch was gentle, it could not be resisted. Scrooge got out of bed. But seeing that the ghost was moving toward the window, he tried to pull away.

"I am only human," Scrooge said, shivering. "I will fall."

"Not while I touch you," said the ghost. "Come."

As he spoke these words, the ghost and Scrooge passed through the wall. Suddenly, they were standing on a country road. The city streets had vanished, along with the darkness and mist. It was a cold, clear, winter day, and there was snow on the ground.

"I know this place!" cried Scrooge. "I was born here." As he looked around him, memories of happy days long ago rushed back into his mind.

"Your lip is trembling," said the ghost. "Is that a tear on your cheek?"

"No!" said Scrooge, wiping it away.

"It is strange that you have forgotten all about this place for so many years," said the ghost. "Let us go on."

As they walked along the road, Scrooge recognized every gate, every post, and every tree. Shaggy ponies came trotting toward them with healthy-looking young boys on their backs. Scrooge knew them and named every one of them. Why was he so pleased to see them? Why did his heart beat so fast and his eyes fill with tears as he heard them call "Merry Christmas!" to each other as they went their separate ways at the crossroads? What was Christmas to Scrooge? What good had it ever done for him?

"There's the school over there," cried Scrooge.

"Yes," said the ghost. "It's not quite empty. A lonely child, who has been forgotten by his friends, is still there."

Scrooge knew who that child was. It was he. They looked in through the window, and there he was, as a young boy, reading near a feeble fire.

Suddenly, a strange man dressed in strange clothing appeared at the window. "Why, it's Ali Baba!" cried Scrooge. "I remember I was reading about him, and there goes Robinson Crusoe and his man Friday."

The picture quickly faded. Scrooge seemed lost in thought. "I wish . . . but it's too late now."

"What is the matter?" asked the spirit.

"Nothing," said Scrooge. "Only there was a boy singing a Christmas carol at my door last night. I wish I had given him something, that's all."

The ghost smiled and waved his hand. "Let us see another Christmas," he said.

The scene changed. It was the same room, only a little darker and dingier. Scrooge saw himself as a boy again. Only he had grown larger by now. Once more, he was alone.

The door opened and a little girl rushed in. Putting her arms around his neck, she kissed him and said, "Dear brother, I have come to take you home."

"Home?" asked the boy in surprise.

"Yes, home!" cried the girl, dancing about the room. "Father sent me in a coach to bring you. We are going to have the merriest Christmas together."

She clapped her hands and laughed, and the boy laughed, too. The boy's luggage was carried down and put into the coach. They climbed in after it and were soon driving away over the frosty roads.

The elderly Scrooge sighed as he watched. "She was so delicate," he said to the ghost, "but her heart was always so warm."

"She lived to be a woman," said the ghost, "and when she died, she left children behind here."

"One child," said Scrooge.

"True," said the ghost. "Your nephew."

CHAPTER FOUR · A CHRISTMAS PARTY

The scene changed again, and the school was left behind. Now Ebenezer Scrooge and the ghost were in the city, with all the windows decorated for Christmas and all the streets lit up. The ghost stopped in front of a warehouse and asked Scrooge if he recognized it.

"Recognize it?" cried Scrooge. "Why, I was an apprentice here."

They went in and found an old gentleman with a wig sitting behind a high desk.

"It's old Fezziwig, bless his heart," said Scrooge. "What a kind man he was!"

Old Fezziwig laid down his pen and looked at the clock, which pointed to seven. He rubbed his hands together and chuckled. Then he shouted in a jovial voice, "Yo ho, there! Ebenezer! Dick!"

The door opened, and Scrooge, as a young man, came in, followed by another apprentice.

"I'm sure that's Dick Wilkins!" said Scrooge. "Good old Dick!"

"No more work tonight, my boys," said Fezziwig, smiling. "This is Christmas Eve. Put up those shutters, my lads. Clear everything out of the way. We'll need plenty of room."

Clear away! There was nothing they wouldn't have cleared away. The floor was swept, more lamps were lit, and more coal heaped on the fire. Soon the warehouse was as snug and bright as any ballroom.

A fiddler came in with a music book and settled himself on a desk. Mrs. Fezziwig came in, bustling and beaming. Next were Fezziwig's three daughters, all blushing and smiling. Then six young men, the housemaid, the cook, the baker, and the milkman all came in. Anyone who had anything to do with the Fezziwigs was welcome.

They danced around the room, twenty couples or more, with old Fezziwig clapping his hands and shouting "Well done!" until the fiddler was worn out. Then there was more dancing and games, then cake and wine, a large roast beef, mince pies, and all sorts of good things to eat.

The party ended as the clock struck eleven. Mr. and Mrs. Fezziwig stood at the door, shaking hands with all of the guests and wishing them a merry Christmas. As the scene faded away, Scrooge sighed with disappointment. He had enjoyed it all so much, just as he had in those days long ago.

"What's the matter?" asked the ghost.

"Nothing really," said Scrooge. "Only I wish I had said a kind word or two to my clerk, Bob Cratchit. That's all."

"My time is running out," said the ghost. "Quick!"

Just then, a new vision appeared. Scrooge saw himself as he had looked in the prime of his life. His face had changed. It had begun to show

lines of worry and of greed.

He was not alone. A young girl sat beside him. She looked at him sadly and said, "You have changed, Ebenezer. Now you care more about money than you care about me. I am poor and cannot make you rich. It would be better for us to part. You were a different man when we were first engaged to be married."

"I was a boy then," he said impatiently.

"And now you are sorry for having promised to marry me. Very well. I will not hold you to your promise. May you be happy in the life you have chosen." She left him, ending their courtship.

"Show me no more," cried Scrooge to the spirit. "I cannot bear it. Why are you torturing me? Take me home."

"One more shadow," said the ghost.

"No more!" cried Scrooge. "I do not want to see any more!"

The scene changed, and this time they saw a room. It was not richly furnished, but still it was cozy. A lovely girl sat near a blazing fire. She was so much like the one in the last scene that Scrooge almost thought she was the same girl. But soon he saw that she herself was sitting across from the

young girl. She had grown into a pleasant older woman, and that young girl was her daughter.

Other children were playing noisy games in the room. Then there was a knocking on the door. The children's father came in, carrying Christmas toys and presents. He was immediately surrounded. The children dove into his pockets and hugged him around his neck. At last, he freed himself and sat down by the fire.

Scrooge's eyes blurred as he watched. He realized then that if it were not for his love of money, he might have been sitting there.

"Spirit," he cried in a faltering voice, "take me away from this place! I cannot stand it! Don't haunt me any longer!"

The light around the ghost's head began to fade. Suddenly, Scrooge was back in his own bedroom. He had barely tumbled into his bed before he fell into a heavy sleep.

CHAPTER FIVE -

THE SECOND OF THE THREE SPIRITS

Scrooge could not tell how long he had been asleep. But when he opened his eyes, the clock struck one again. It was time for the second spirit to appear.

Five minutes, ten minutes, a quarter of an hour went by, and still nothing happened. He noticed, however, that the room was filled with light that seemed to come from next door. He got up and shuffled to the door in his slippers.

The moment Scrooge's hand touched the doorknob, a strange voice called his name and told him to enter. Scrooge obeyed.

It was his own room—there was no doubt about that. But greenery and branches were hung from the ceiling and on the walls so that the room looked like a forest. Holly, mistletoe, and red berries reflected the light of a huge fire blazing in the fireplace.

Turkeys, geese, poultry, roasts of meat, long strings of sausages, mince pies, plum puddings, roasted chestnuts, rosy red apples, juicy oranges, and steaming bowls of punch were heaped on the floor to form a kind of throne. Sitting on top of this mountain of Christmas food was a jolly giant. The giant held a glowing torch up high to shed light on Scrooge as he poked his nose around the door.

"Come in!" cried the ghost in hearty welcome. "Come in and get to know me better."

Scrooge entered timidly.

"I am the Ghost of Christmas Present," said the spirit. "Come, look at me!"

Scrooge looked up and saw that the spirit was dressed in a deep green cape trimmed with white fur. He wore a wreath of holly on his head, with icicles hanging from it.

"Touch my cape," said the spirit.

Scrooge did as he was told. Instantly, the holly, mistletoe, berries, and Christmas food vanished. So did the room, the fire, and all sense of time. Now they stood in a city street on Christmas morning.

The ghost led Scrooge through streets where all of the people seemed to be very poor but still full of the joy of Christmas. At last, they reached a very humble house where Scrooge's clerk, Bob Cratchit, lived with his wife and family.

Although Bob's weekly wages were very low, the Cratchits were celebrating Christmas in as festive a manner as they could. Mrs. Cratchit was laying the tablecloth with the help of her daughter, Belinda. The oldest son, Peter, was testing the potatoes with a fork to see if they were done. Two smaller Cratchits came tearing in to say that they had smelled their goose, which was now cooking at the baker's.

"Here I am, Mother!" cried a girl, appearing at the door.

"It's Martha!" cried the two young Cratchits. "We've got such a goose, Martha!"

"My goodness, dear, you are very late," said Mrs. Cratchit, kissing her oldest daughter a dozen times and taking off her shawl and bonnet.

"We had such a lot of work to finish off at the shop. I couldn't get away," said Martha.

"Sit down in front of the fire and get warmed up."

"No, no! Here's father coming," cried the young Cratchits. "Hide, Martha, hide!"

So Martha playfully hid herself. In came Bob Cratchit, with his old clothing tidied up for the occasion and Tiny Tim perched on his shoulder. Tiny Tim was lame and had to carry a crutch. But he was everybody's favorite and a brave little fellow in spite of his handicap.

"Where's Martha?" asked Bob Cratchit, looking around the room.

"She's not coming," said his wife.

"Not coming?" said Bob, looking as if his heart would break. "Not coming on Christmas Day?"

Martha could not stand to see him looking so disappointed, so she came out from behind the closet door and hugged him tightly.

"How did Tiny Tim behave in church?" asked Mrs. Cratchit, after Bob had hugged Martha to his heart's content.

"As good as gold," said Bob, "and better."

Bob kept busy making a hot mixture in a jug with sugar, water, and lemons, stirring it around and around and then setting it over the fire to simmer. Soon Peter and the two young Cratchits went off to pick up the goose and then proudly carried it back.

At last, everything was ready. The family bowed their heads and said grace. Then Mrs. Cratchit carved the goose. As she served the stuffing, there was a murmur of delight from everyone. Even Tiny Tim beat his knife on the table and feebly cried, "Hurray!"

There had never been another goose that was quite as marvelous as this one! There was plenty for everyone, including loads of applesauce and mounds of mashed potatoes.

After the goose and side dishes had been eaten, Belinda cleared away the dirty plates and then set clean ones. Mrs. Cratchit left the room and proudly brought in the pudding. It looked like a speckled cannonball and was decorated with a sprig of holly stuck on top.

It was wonderful pudding! Bob Cratchit said it was the greatest success achieved by Mrs. Cratchit since their marriage. Everybody had something to say about it. And although it was a very small pudding for such a large family, not one of them complained because they knew they couldn't afford a bigger one.

Every last spoonful was eaten. Then the table was cleared, the hearth was swept, and the fire was built up. Apples and oranges were put on the table, and a bucket full of chestnuts was placed on the fire. The mixture of sugar, water, and lemons in the jug was tasted, and everyone agreed it was perfect.

"Merry Christmas to all, my dears. God bless us!" said Bob Cratchit.

"God bless us, every one!" said Tiny Tim.

He sat very close to his father on his little stool. Bob held Tiny Tim's frail hand tightly in his, as if he was afraid that Tim might be taken away from him.

Scrooge turned toward the ghost. "Spirit," he said, "tell me if Tiny Tim will live."

"I see an empty chair," said the ghost, "and a crutch without an owner. If these shadows remain unchanged, the child will die."

"No, no!" cried Scrooge. "Say he will live!"

"If he is to die, he had better do it. You said yourself that there were too many poor people!"

Scrooge lowered his head, filled with grief and shame. Then suddenly, he heard his own name being spoken.

"Mr. Scrooge," said Bob Cratchit, raising his glass. "I'll give a toast to Mr. Scrooge. The wages he pays me made this feast possible."

"The wages he pays you indeed!" said Mrs. Cratchit, growing angry. "I'd give him a piece of my mind if I had him here."

"My dear!" said Bob. "This is Christmas Day."

"Nobody knows better than you how stingy, heartless, and unfeeling he is," said his wife.

But again Bob said gently, "My dear! Christmas Day."

"Oh, all right," said Mrs. Cratchit. "I'll drink to his health for your sake and Christmas Day's, but not for his. Merry Christmas to him! I have no doubt he'll be very merry!"

Scrooge was the ogre of the Cratchit family. Even just mentioning his name threw a dark shadow over the party. It took nearly five minutes before the shadow was lifted again.

When it had passed away, they were ten times merrier than before from the sheer relief that they had finished with Scrooge. Martha told them stories about all the fine people who came into the store where she worked. As she spoke, the roasted chestnuts and the jug were passed around and around. By and by, Tiny Tim sang them a song. And the day passed on with the family growing closer and closer to each other in happiness and comfort.

Scrooge did not want to leave the peaceful scene. His eyes rested on all of them, but mostly on Tiny Tim. When the ghost led him away, Scrooge could still see the pale face and hear the feeble voice saying, "God bless us, every one!"

CHAPTER SIX - PEACE ON EARTH

It was getting dark and snowing heavily by the time Scrooge and the spirit left the Cratchits' humble house. And now, without a word of warning from the ghost, they stood in a bleak field.

"Where are we?" asked Scrooge, shivering.

"This is a place where miners live," said the ghost. "They work deep in the earth."

A light shone from the windows of a hut. The ghost made his way toward it and passed inside. Here, Scrooge saw a cheerful group of people gathered around a blazing fire. They were singing Christmas carols as happily as anyone could. Even in this deserted place, Christmas was not forgotten.

The ghost did not stay here very long. He made Scrooge take hold of his cape, saying they were going to travel out to the sea. Scrooge was horrified when he saw the rocks ahead and heard the thunder of the water rolling toward the coast. But the ghost led him onward, and he had to follow.

At last, they reached a solitary lighthouse high up on some rocks on a deserted coast. The two men who kept the light burning, a light that warned passing ships of danger, had made a fire. They were shaking hands and wishing each other a merry Christmas. Then they began to sing. Their song was like a gale of wind itself. Christmas had found its way even to a lonely lighthouse.

Next, Scrooge and the spirit went away to a ship. They stood beside the man at the wheel, the officers on watch, and all the men doing their different chores. Every one of them was humming a Christmas tune, thinking about Christmas, or speaking about some past Christmas Day spent at home.

Suddenly, Scrooge was surprised to hear a hearty laugh and to recognize that it was his own nephew's. Even more surprising, he found that he was now in a bright room of a house where his nephew, Fred, was at a party with his friends.

"Ha, ha!" laughed Fred. "He said that Christmas was a humbug. He believed it, too!"

"Well then, shame on him, Fred," said his wife. She was very pretty, with a cheerful face and the shiniest pair of eyes you ever saw.

"He's a strange old fellow," said Scrooge's nephew, "and not pleasant at times. However, I can't say anything against him."

"He must be very rich," said his wife.

"Yes, I know. But money's no use to him. He doesn't do any good with it."

"I have no patience with him," said his wife.

"Oh, I have," said Fred. "I feel sorry for him. Who pays the price for his grumpy behavior? He does. He has made up his mind to dislike us and won't come and have dinner with us. What's the result? He loses a good dinner." And he laughed out loud at the thought of it.

"You're a silly fellow," said his wife, laughing at him.

"But it's true," said Fred. "I am sure his own thoughts, his moldy office, or his dismal house cannot be very pleasant. However, I am going to give him the same chance every year whether he likes it or not. Maybe one day, I might even get him in the mood to give poor Bob Cratchit a raise."

Fred laughed again, and everyone laughed with him. Before long, they had some music. Fred's wife played the harp beautifully, and the others sang carols and songs that Scrooge remembered from his childhood.

But they did not spend the whole evening making music. They played all kinds of party games. There must have been twenty people present, young and old, and they all joined in. Scrooge begged to stay at the party until they had played another game.

It was called "Yes or No." Scrooge's nephew had to think of something, and the rest had to find out what it was. They asked him questions that he could only answer by saying yes or no. They tried everything under the sun. When someone asked, "Is it a bear?" Scrooge's nephew roared with laughter. His wife's plump sister cried, "I know what it is. It's your uncle Scrooge!"

"Right!" said Fred. "And he has given us so much to laugh at, it would be ungrateful not to drink a toast to his health."

"Uncle Scrooge!" they all cried and lifted their glasses.

"Merry Christmas to him, wherever he is," said Fred.

Scrooge would have stayed to thank the company in a speech they could not have heard, but the spirit dragged him off once more on their travels.

They went far away and saw many things. Christmas had left its blessing everywhere, and Scrooge could hardly believe that people with so many troubles and so little money could be so happy.

It was a long night – if, in fact, it did happen all in one night. Scrooge had his doubts about it, for they saw so much and traveled so far. Suddenly, he noticed that the ghost seemed to have grown old and tired. "Are spirits' lives always that short?" Scrooge asked in surprise.

"My life ends tonight at midnight. Listen! The time is coming closer."

Just then, Scrooge saw two figures kneeling at the spirit's feet. They were two children, wretched, ragged, and starving.

Scrooge gasped in horror. "Spirit, are they yours?" he asked.

"They are man's," said the spirit. "This boy is Ignorance. This girl is Poverty."

"Can anything be done to help them?" cried Scrooge.

"Are there no prisons?" said the spirit, throwing Scrooge's own words back in his face. "Are there no workhouses?"

A bell struck twelve. As the last chime faded away, the spirit vanished.

CHAPTER SEVEN - THE LAST OF THE SPIRITS

Slowly, the third and last ghost drew near to Scrooge, and the air seemed full of mystery and gloom. The spirit wore a black garment that hid his face and his shape. Nothing was showing except one hand.

"Are you the Ghost of Christmas Future?" asked Scrooge, shaking. The spirit pointed onward with his hand and slowly nodded his head. That was the only answer he gave.

"Ghost of the future," cried Scrooge, "I am more afraid of you than any other spirit I have seen. But I know your purpose is to teach me to live to be a better man. Lead on, and I will follow you."

The ghost moved away. Scrooge followed in his shadow, which seemed to carry him along. In less than a moment, they were in the business section of the city. The spirit stopped beside a group of men. Scrooge stood near them to listen.

"When did he die?" asked one of the men.

"Last night," said another. "I wonder what he has done with his money?"

"He hasn't left any to me. That's all I know," said a third.

The group of men laughed at this joke. "It's likely to be a very small funeral," said one. "I can't think of a single person who will go to it. Why don't we all go together?"

"If there's a good lunch provided, I might consider it," said another.

Scrooge knew them and wondered who the dead man they were discussing could be.

Standing quietly by his side, the spirit pointed onward again with his outstretched hand. Scrooge had the feeling that the ghost's hidden eyes were watching every move he made. It made him shudder and feel very cold.

Leaving this busy scene, they went next to a part of town where Scrooge had never been before. The streets were narrow and dirty, the shops and houses were wretched, and the people were ragged. The whole place was full of horrible smells, filth, and misery.

The spirit stopped at a store where iron, old rags, bottles, and scrap metal were bought. An old man with gray hair was calmly sitting beside a charcoal stove.

A woman trudged into the shop. Scrooge saw that it was the old woman who kept his dismal rooms tidy. She put down her bundle and winked at the old man.

"Taken from your dead master, I'll bet," he said with a chuckle.

"And why not?" she said. "He can't use them now. Besides, if he had been a better person while he was alive, somebody would have looked after him when he was dying."

"It's his own fault," agreed the old man. "Open the bundle."

Scrooge staggered back in shock as he saw his own belongings dumped out.

Then the scene changed again. Scrooge nearly jumped out of his shoes, for now he found himself next to a bed on which the dead man lay.

"Spirit," said Scrooge, shivering from head to foot, "I see the lesson you want to teach me. This is how my own life might end unless I change my ways."

The ghost spread his dark cloak like a wing, and suddenly they were in a room that Scrooge recognized as Bob Cratchit's. Mrs. Cratchit and the children were sitting around the fire, trying to be cheerful. Everyone was trying not to notice that Tiny Tim's chair was empty.

"It must be about time for your father to come home," said Mrs. Cratchit.

"Past it," said Peter. "But I think he has been walking home a little more slowly than usual lately."

They were quiet again. Then Mrs. Cratchit said, in a voice that trembled a little, "I have seen him walk very quickly with Tiny Tim on his shoulder. But then, Tiny Tim was very light to carry, and it was no trouble to Bob."

At that moment, Bob Cratchit came in. Mrs. Cratchit hurried to greet him.

The two young Cratchits climbed on his knees, hugged him, and said, "Please don't be sad, Father."

Bob was cheerful with them. But his eyes strayed to Tiny Tim's empty chair, and it was difficult to keep back the tears.

"I met Mr. Scrooge's nephew today," he said, moving closer to the fire. "He gave me his card and told me to come to him if I needed help. He doesn't have much money himself, I know, but it was the thought that counts. It almost seemed as if he had known our Tiny Tim himself and knew just how we felt."

"I'm sure he's a good man," said Mrs. Cratchit.

"He said he would try to get Peter a job."

"And then," said one of the younger children, "Peter will be dating girls and leaving us."

"What nonsense!" said Peter, grinning.

"I am sure you will, Peter," said Bob. "There's plenty of time for that. But whenever any of you do leave home, I am sure none of you will forget Tiny Tim, who was the first to leave us."

"Never, Father!" they all cried.

"And I know," he went on, "that we will always remember how patient and good he was."

"We will always remember," they promised.

"Spirit," begged Scrooge, "take me away. I cannot stand to watch any more."

A moment later, Scrooge found himself in an overgrown cemetery. The spirit stood among the old gravestones and pointed silently to one.

Scrooge walked closer to it. Then, in a shudder of horror, he saw the name EBENEZER SCROOGE. He fell to his knees, crying, "Am I the man who lay upon that bed?"

The spirit pointed from the grave to him, and back again.

"No, spirit, no! Tell me I can change these shadows! I am not the man I was. Tell me this does not have to be!"

Just then, the ghost's hood and dress began to change. They shrank, collapsed, and faded until they finally turned into a bedpost.

CHAPTER EIGHT - THE END OF IT

The bedpost was Scrooge's own. The bed was his own. The room was his own.

"Heaven be praised!" cried Scrooge, scrambling from bed. "I am alive and still have time to make up for the past. I will never forget the lesson the three spirits have taught me."

He was so full of good intentions and so excited that he hardly knew what he was doing. He went rushing into the living room in such high spirits that he almost knocked himself out.

"There's the pot with the broth in it," he said, looking around the room. "There's the door where the ghost of Jacob Marley came in. It is all right. It's all true. It all happened. Ha, ha, ha!"

For a man who had been out of practice for so many years, it was a splendid laugh. And it was only the first of many.

"I don't know what day of the month it is," said Scrooge. "I don't know how long I've been away with the spirits. I don't know anything!"

Just then, the church bells rang out the loudest, most glorious chimes he had ever heard. He ran to the window, opened it, and stuck his head out. The fog and mist had gone, and the air was clear and cold. There was golden sunlight and a heavenly sky. The air was fresh and sweet, and merry bells rang everywhere.

"What day is it today?" shouted Scrooge to a boy below, who was dressed in his Sunday clothes.

"What?" said the boy. "Why, it's Christmas Day!"

"It's Christmas Day!" said Scrooge to himself in great delight. "I haven't missed it. The spirits have done it all in one night. Excuse me, my fine young man!"

"What?" said the boy.

"Do you know the butcher shop down at the corner?"

"Of course, I do," said the boy.

"A clever boy," said Scrooge. "A remarkable boy! Do you know if they have sold the prize turkey that was hanging in the window yet?"

"You mean the one that's the same size as I am?" asked the boy.

"Yes, my boy, the big one."

"It's hanging there now."

"Go and buy it," said Scrooge. "Go and buy it, and tell them to bring it here. Come back with the man, and I'll give you a shilling."

The boy took off like a shot.

"I'll have it sent to Bob Cratchit," said Scrooge, rubbing his hands and laughing at the thought of it. "He won't know who sent it. It's twice the size of Tiny Tim."

Scrooge's hand was trembling with excitement as he wrote the address. Then he went downstairs to the street door to wait for the turkey.

It was a gigantic turkey. It was so enormous that it seemed it could never have stood up by itself on its own legs.

"It would be impossible to carry that all the way to Bob Cratchit's," said Scrooge to the man from the butcher shop. "You must have a cab."

He chuckled when he said this, and he chuckled when he paid for the turkey. He chuckled when he paid for the cab to take the man and the turkey in. And he chuckled when he gave the boy his money.

Scrooge went out in the street. By this time, there were people everywhere. Scrooge greeted everyone he saw with a delightful smile. He looked so pleasant that some of them stopped to say, "Good morning, sir. Merry Christmas!"

He had not gone far when he saw one of the gentlemen who had come into his office the day before. It was the same man he had turned away empty-handed.

"My dear sir," said Scrooge, stopping and shaking the gentleman's hand. "Merry Christmas to you!"

"Mr. Scrooge!" said the man in surprise.

"Yes," said Scrooge. "That is my name. I am afraid it may not be a pleasant one to you. Allow me to ask your pardon. And will you have the goodness to accept — " Here, Scrooge whispered something in his ear.

"Good heavens!" cried the gentleman. "Are you serious?"

"I am, and I intend to donate that amount and not a penny less," said Scrooge.

"My dear sir," said the gentleman, shaking hands with him, "I don't

know what to say."

"Don't say anything, please," said Scrooge. "Come and see me tomorrow."

"I will!" cried the gentleman.

"Thank you," said Scrooge. "I am much obliged to you. God bless you!"

The next thing Scrooge did was to go to church. Then he walked through the streets, patting children on the head, speaking to beggars, and finding that everything gave him a wonderfully warm feeling.

In the afternoon, Scrooge headed for his nephew's house. He passed the door half a dozen times before he could get up enough courage to knock.

"Is your master at home, my dear?" Scrooge asked the maid who opened the door.

"Yes, sir. I'll show you into the parlor if you please."

"Thank you. He knows me," said Scrooge with his hand on the dining room door.

He turned the handle and poked his head around the door. There sat his nephew and niece, ready to begin their meal.

"Fred!" said Scrooge.

"I can't believe it!" cried Fred. "What are you doing here?"

"I have come for dinner. Will you let me in, Fred?"

"Let you in? Why, Uncle, of course!"

It took less than five minutes for Scrooge to feel right at home. Fred's wife was just as glad to see him. So was her plump sister when she came, and all the other guests when they arrived. It was a wonderful party, filled with games, fun, and happiness.

The next morning, Scrooge arrived at his office very early. If only he could be there first and catch Bob Cratchit coming late!

Bob was a full eighteen and a half minutes late. Scrooge sat with his door wide open so that he would see Bob go into his room.

Bob Cratchit's hat was off before he opened the door. He was at his desk in a twinkling, scribbling away with his pen, trying to make up for lost time.

"Hello!" growled Scrooge, as near to his usual gruff voice as he could make it. "What do you mean by coming here at this time of day?"

"I am very sorry, sir," said Bob.

"I'll tell you what," said Scrooge, "I am not going to stand it any longer. And therefore," he said, pausing for effect, "and therefore, I am going to give you a raise."

Bob Cratchit shook. For a moment, he thought Scrooge had lost his mind. Bob even had an idea of knocking Scrooge down and running for help.

But Ebenezer Scrooge was as good as his word. He gave Bob Cratchit a raise—and did a great deal more. He became a second father to Tiny Tim, who did not die. Scrooge was as good a friend, as good a boss, and as good a man as the old city or any other city had ever seen. Some people laughed at the way he had changed. But he let them laugh and did not pay any attention to them. His own heart laughed, and that was quite enough for him.

Later, it was always said of Scrooge that he knew how to celebrate Christmas as well as any man alive. May that be truly said of all of us. And as Tiny Tim observed, "God bless us, every one!"

Joyfully

Deck the halls with boughs of hol-ly, Fa la la la la, la la la la. 'Tis the sea-son to be jol-ly, Fa la la la la, la la la la. Don we now our gay ap-par-el Fa la la, la la la, la la la. Troll the an-cient Yule-tide car-ol, Fa la la la la, la la la la

Deck the Halls

2. See the blazing Yule before us,
Fa la la la la, la la la la.
Strike the harp and join the chorus,
Fa la la la la, la la la la.
Follow me in merry measure,
Fa la la, la la la, la la la.
While I tell of Yuletide treasure,
Fa la la la la, la la la la.

3. Fast away the old year passes,
Fa la la la la, la la la la.
Hail the new, ye lads and lasses,
Fa la la la la, la la la la.
Sing we joyous all together,
Fa la la, la la la, la la la.
Heedless of the wind and weather,
Fa la la la la, la la la la.

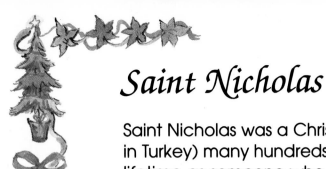

Saint Nicholas

Saint Nicholas was a Christian bishop. He lived in the city of Myra (now in Turkey) many hundreds of years ago. Nicholas was well known in his lifetime as someone who liked to do good. He especially liked to help people secretly.

There is one famous legend about Saint Nicholas. The story tells of Nicholas hearing one day of three beautiful sisters who lived in a miserable hut on the edge of Myra.

The three sisters were very poor. They could barely earn enough to keep themselves and their old mother from starving to death. When Nicholas heard of their plight, he was very concerned. He decided to do something to help them.

One night, when everyone was asleep, Nicholas crept through the streets to the edge of town. Quietly, he tiptoed up to the hut where the three sisters lived. He climbed onto the roof and dropped three bags of gold through the hole in the roof where the smoke from the fire came out.

Now it so happened that the three sisters had washed their stockings before they went to bed. The stockings had been hung by the fire to dry. When Nicholas dropped the gold through the smoke hole, each bag of gold fell into a stocking.

The three sisters were overjoyed to find bags of gold in their stockings when they woke up the next morning. Soon, the story began to spread. Other people began to hang up stockings in the hope of finding bags of gold when they woke up in the morning.

From this legend sprang the custom of hanging stockings up by the chimney on Christmas Eve. Over the years, Saint Nicholas became associated with Christmas. In some cultures, he is a jolly man named Santa Claus. In other cultures, he is still a kindly bishop or saint.

Santa Claus Around the World

Children in countries around the world await a visit from a mysterious bringer of gifts at Christmas time. He is always a kindly man who brings them toys, other presents, or money. We know him as Santa Claus, but in many other countries he is called by other names.

Giving people presents at Christmas is a very ancient custom that has been followed for hundreds of years. During the Roman midwinter feast days, people exchanged gifts. They did it again on New Year's Day, and the gifts that they gave to each other were thought to bring luck for the New Year ahead. When Christianity spread throughout the world, the custom of giving presents continued. The gift-giving feast was called Christmas.

In many countries, the person who brings the gifts at Christmas time comes at night. This person leaves the presents for children to find the next morning. However, in other countries, the bringer of gifts arrives during the day, often with an assistant who helps him distribute them.

In some European countries, the bringer of gifts is Saint Nicholas of Myra. He arrives on the eve of his feast day (December 5), on a day in Advent (the season just before Christmas), or on Christmas Eve itself. When he arrives, he is wearing his bishop's robes and his miter (a tall, pointed hat). He brings a strange-looking crew of followers with him. These people are often wearing masks and unusual clothing. In the Netherlands, Saint Nicholas's helper is called Black Peter. His job is to make sure that children have been good throughout the year and to help Saint Nicholas give away the presents.

In parts of Germany, children write

letters to the baby Jesus with their Christmas present list. In Spain, children are given gifts on the feast of Epiphany (when Christians celebrate the arrival of the Magi, or three wise men, in Bethlehem to see the baby Jesus). They leave their shoes on the windowsills of the houses to be filled by the wise men as they ride past.

The bringer of gifts in North America is Santa Claus. He's a fat, jolly man with a white beard who arrives on Christmas Eve in a sleigh pulled by flying reindeer. Children will sometimes leave snacks for Santa to help him on his journey. Stockings are hung by the chimney or elsewhere in the hope that Santa will fill them with little presents and goodies. And children especially look forward to waking up on Christmas Day and finding underneath the Christmas tree even bigger presents left by Santa.

O Christmas Tree

2. O Christmas tree, O Christmas tree,
Thou hast a wondrous message.
O Christmas tree, O Christmas tree,
Thou hast a wondrous message.
Thou dost proclaim the Savior's birth,
Good will to men and peace on earth.
O Christmas tree, O Christmas tree,
Thou hast a wondrous message.

3. O Christmas Tree, O Christmas Tree,
You glow with Christmas brightness.
O Christmas Tree, O Christmas Tree,
We sing with joyful lightness.
The radiance of this happy night,
To all of us gives hope and light,
O Christmas Tree,O Christmas Tree,
You glow with Christmas brightness.

The Story of the Christmas Tree

People often wonder where the custom of having a tree in the home during Christmas time comes from. We will probably never know for sure. But there are several historical clues that point out where this custom came from.

An Ancient Symbol

Thousands of years ago, there were people who believed that evergreen trees were magical. Even in winter, when all the other trees and greenery were brown and bare, the evergreen stayed strong and green. People saw the evergreen as a symbol of life and as a sure sign that sunshine and spring would soon return. Candles, or the electric lights we use to decorate our trees today, are also an ancient symbol. They represent the light of spring triumphing over the darkness of winter.

In ancient Rome, people decorated their homes and their temples with greenery during a special December feast. It was a happy time. No battles could be fought, the schools were closed, and people everywhere joined in the carnival-like atmosphere and gave each other presents.

The Modern Tree

So when did the Christmas tree go indoors? Legend has it that the tradition was begun by Martin Luther in Germany. He was a monk and church reformer who lived from 1483 to 1546. According to the legend, Luther was returning home one wintry night when he saw the stars twinkling in the sky through the tree branches. Luther was amazed by the sight, and when he arrived home, he was eager to tell his family about it. To help them understand, he went to the woods and cut down a small fir tree. Luther brought it indoors and decorated it with candles, which represented the stars he had seen.

The custom spread in Germany, and from there all over the world. In England, the Christmas tree first appeared when Queen Victoria married Prince Albert, who was German. In 1841, Albert set up a Christmas tree at Windsor Castle near London to remind him of his homeland. The Christmas tree custom was brought to the United States by people from England as well as by many German immigrants who came in the 1800s. Whatever its origin, the Christmas tree is a beautiful symbol for everyone who celebrates Christmas.

GROWING YOUR OWN MINIATURE CHRISTMAS TREE

Would you like to grow your own miniature Christmas tree? It's easy! You can even grow several and use them as decorations around your house.

WHAT YOU NEED

Pine cone

A small plastic container

Water

Dirt

Grass seed

How to grow your own Christmas tree:

Make sure that the bottom of the pine cone is flat and that the cone will stand up. If there is a stem, break it off.

Soak the pine cone in water for a while until it is completely wet. Then take it out of the water.

Fill the bottom of the small plastic container with about half an inch (one and a half centimeters) of water.

Stand the pine cone in the water and sprinkle it with dirt.

Put some grass seed all over the pine cone. Make sure that the seed is evenly placed.

Leave your pine cone someplace where it will get lots of light. A sunny windowsill is a good spot. Keep checking to see that there is still some water in the container— about the same amount you started with.

In a week or so, the grass seed will grow, and your pine cone will sprout green. When it has a chance to grow a bit, trim the greenery with scissors. Now you have your own miniature Christmas tree!

The Twelve Days of Christmas

Brightly

F   Gm   C7   F

1. On the first day of Christ-mas, my true love gave to me   A

B♭   F/C   C7   F

par-tridge__ in a pear   tree. 2. On the sec-ond day of Christ-mas, my

Gm   C7   F   Gm   C7   F   B♭   F/C   C7

true love gave to me   Two tur-tle-doves and a par-tridge__ in a pear

F   Gm   C7   F

tree.   3. On the third day of Christ-mas, my true love gave to me

C7   F   B♭   F/C   C7

Three French hens, two tur-tle-doves, and a par-tridge___ in a pear

tree. 4. On the fourth day of Christ-mas my true love gave to me

Four call-ing birds, three French hens, two tur-tle-doves, and a

par - tridge__ in a pear tree. 5. On the fifth day of Christ-mas, my

true love gave to me Five gold-en rings, four call-ing birds,

three French hens, two tur-tle-doves, and a par-tridge__ in a pear

tree. 6. On the sixth
seventh
eighth
ninth
tenth
eleventh
twelfth } day of Christmas, my true love gave to me

Six geese a-lay-ing, five golden rings,
Seven swans a-swim-ming,
Eight maids a-milk-ing,
Nine la-dies danc-ing,
Ten lords a-leap-ing,
Eleven pip-ers pip-ing,
Twelve drum-mers drumming,

four call-ing birds, three French hens, two tur-tle-doves, and a

par-tridge__ in a pear tree. 7.On the tree.

* Repeat this bar in reverse order as necessary.

58

The Twelve Days of Christmas

On the first day of Christmas,
my true love gave to me
A partridge in a pear tree.

On the second day of Christmas,
my true love gave to me
Two turtledoves and a partridge in a
pear tree.

On the third day of Christmas,
my true love gave to me
Three French hens, two turtledoves,
and a partridge in a pear tree.

On the fourth day of Christmas,
my true love gave to me
Four calling birds, three French hens,
two turtledoves, and a partridge in a
pear tree.

On the fifth day of Christmas,
my true love gave to me
Five golden rings, four calling birds,
three French hens, two turtledoves,
and a partridge in a pear tree.

On the sixth day of Christmas,
my true love gave to me
Six geese a-laying, five golden rings,
four calling birds, three French hens,
two turtledoves, and a partridge in a
pear tree.

On the seventh day of Christmas,
my true love gave to me
Seven swans a-swimming, six geese
a-laying, five golden rings, four calling
birds, three French hens, two turtledoves, and a partridge in a pear tree.

On the eighth day of Christmas,
my true love gave to me
Eight maids a-milking, seven swans

a-swimming, six geese a-laying, five
golden rings, four calling birds, three
French hens, two turtledoves, and a
partridge in a pear tree.

On the ninth day of Christmas,
my true love gave to me
Nine ladies dancing, eight maids
a-milking, seven swans a-swimming, six
geese a-laying, five golden rings, four
calling birds, three French hens, two
turtledoves, and a partridge in a pear
tree.

On the tenth day of Christmas,
my true love gave to me
Ten lords a-leaping, nine ladies
dancing, eight maids a-milking, seven
swans a-swimming, six geese a-laying,
five golden rings, four calling birds,
three French hens, two turtledoves,
and a partridge in a pear tree.

On the eleventh day of Christmas,
my true love gave to me
Eleven pipers piping, ten lords
a-leaping, nine ladies dancing, eight
maids a-milking, seven swans
a-swimming, six geese a-laying, five
golden rings, four calling birds, three
French hens, two turtledoves, and a
partridge in a pear tree.

On the twelfth day of Christmas,
my true love gave to me
Twelve drummers drumming, eleven
pipers piping, ten lords a-leaping, nine
ladies dancing, eight maids a-milking,
seven swans a-swimming, six geese
a-laying, five golden rings, four calling
birds, three French hens, two turtledoves, and a partridge in a pear tree.

The Nutcracker

Christmas Eve had finally arrived in the Stahlbaum house. For weeks, everybody had been preparing for the big day. The Christmas cake had been baked, the cookies had been made and set out on fancy plates, and the house was decorated festively from top to bottom.

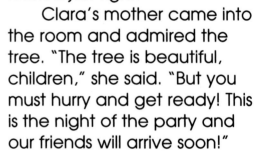

The Christmas tree had also been put up and decorated. What a tree it was! To Clara Stahlbaum, it seemed as if there were a thousand candles on it. Each one was a pinpoint of light. The golden angels and the shiny red and silver balls caught the light from the candle flames and sparkled merrily.

Clara and her brother, Fritz, had trimmed the tree themselves. How exciting it was to take a golden angel or ball out of the box where it had been for a year, then hang it on the tree — hang it in a spot that looked just right.

Clara's mother came into the room and admired the tree. "The tree is beautiful, children," she said. "But you must hurry and get ready! This is the night of the party and our friends will arrive soon!"

Clara and Fritz dressed in their best party clothes. As they did, music from the town band began to float up from the street.

"Oh, Clara, come and see!" called Fritz. "The band is outside, and it has started to snow!"

Clara rushed to the window. Outside, the town bandsmen in their red and gold uniforms were playing a carol. The snowflakes drifted by the window, transforming the street below into a magical kingdom.

"Come on, Clara!" shouted Fritz. "Let's go and see them up close."

The two children ran down the stairs and tugged at the big front door. It swung open, and there stood the first guests to arrive for the Christmas Eve party.

Clara and Fritz waited in the front hallway. The fire blazed brightly as more guests arrived. Soon, the house was filled with adults and children. Then their old family friend, Herr Drosselmeyer, arrived. His arms were full of presents for the family, and his eyes twinkled.

"Hello, my dears! Hello!" he boomed. "Merry Christmas Eve!"

Clara and Fritz were allowed to open the presents that Herr Drosselmeyer had brought. The first one made them gasp with delight. It was a miniature puppet theater for both of them, complete with jointed marionettes that moved and danced when their old friend pulled on the strings. There was also a whole regiment of red-coated toy soldiers for Fritz.

There was a separate present for Clara, too. The wrapping paper was in beautiful colors, and as she undid the ribbon, she wondered what it could possibly be. *Something very special,* she thought, as she started to open the box. Inside, under layers of tissue paper, was a large and very beautiful nutcracker doll. He had a wonderful white, red, and gold uniform and a very handsome face. He had fur trim on his uniform and hat, and shiny medals on his coat. Clara loved

him at once.

"He's wonderful," Clara said breathlessly.

"You must look after him carefully, Clara," said Herr Drosselmeyer. "He's magic."

"I will. I promise, Herr Drosselmeyer," said Clara.

"Come on, Clara!" shouted Fritz. "Carl is here. Let's play upstairs!"

The two boys rushed upstairs, followed by Clara. Soon, the boys began to play a rough wrestling game, forgetting all about Clara. Clara looked at her other presents, placed carefully on a table in the corner of the room. Suddenly, there was a loud crash, and Clara's nutcracker lay on the floor with one arm broken off!

"You've broken it!" shrieked Clara. "You've broken my nutcracker!" She began to cry.

Alerted by the sounds of sobbing upstairs, the children's mother and Herr Drosselmeyer came running into the room.

"Children, children!" cried their mother. "What is wrong?"

"That awful Fritz has broken my nutcracker!" said Clara, sobbing and cradling her broken doll.

"Don't worry, Clara," whispered Herr Drosselmeyer. "It will be all right. I'll mend him for you. Go to bed now. It's late. Wait and see how he is in the morning." Herr Drosselmeyer kissed Clara good night, and off she went to bed.

Clara tried to go to sleep, but she lay awake crying and worrying about her nutcracker. After a while, she got out of bed, put on her robe and slippers, and went downstairs to see her broken toy.

What a sight she saw! Mice were scampering about everywhere, tearing and chewing at all the presents under the Christmas tree. Soon, the room was filled with an army of mice.

Clara looked on in horror. Then she heard someone call, "Over here, men! Ready to charge!" It was her little nutcracker, leading the toy soldiers into battle against the mice.

Suddenly, a fierce-looking mouse, larger than all the rest, appeared. He wore a golden crown and waved a sword of shining steel. It was the Mouse King, and against him the toy soldiers were powerless.

The nutcracker did not give up. He fought bravely, but it was no use. The Mouse King began to get the better of him. Thinking quickly,

63

Clara took off one of her slippers and threw it at the Mouse King with all her might. This startled him, and the nutcracker quickly closed in with his sword. Soon, the Mouse King lay dead. The other mice ran back to their holes.

Clara turned to the nutcracker – only to find that he had been transformed into a handsome young prince.

"Thank you, little Clara," he said smiling. "You have saved my life and broken an evil spell."

Without warning, mist began to swirl wildly around. Suddenly, there was snow everywhere, with thousands of snowflakes floating down from the sky. It seemed to Clara that the snowflakes were dancing.

Then Clara and the prince found themselves on a magical ship with silver sails. They were sailing on a sea of lemonade.

"Where are we going?" she asked.

"Back to my country, the Kingdom of Sweets," the prince replied.

"There, we will meet the Sugar Plum Fairy."

Clara and the prince arrived at a big, beautiful palace. It was filled with people from all corners of the world. They had all come to see the brave Clara, who had saved the life of the prince. Clara and the prince were led into a magnificent room, where a huge feast was laid out. At the head of the table was the beautiful Sugar Plum Fairy herself.

Many different people brought Clara and the prince all sorts of wonderful food. First came Spanish dancers, carrying bowls and baskets of exotic fruits. Then Arabs, clad in rich silks and satins, brought coffee and chocolate. After that, a Chinese boy and girl offered Clara almonds and jasmine tea.

Enchanted, Clara watched as garlands of flowers strung around the palace floated down from the ceiling. As they fell to the marble floor, each flower turned into a dancer wearing a brightly colored costume. Then, as if a breeze had blown through the hall, they were scattered.

Clara hoped the wonderful party would never end. But a glittering sleigh, pulled by reindeer, arrived to take her and the prince away. The Sugar Plum Fairy and all the other people waved good-bye as Clara and the prince soared into the sky, leaving the Kingdom of Sweets behind.

The next thing Clara knew, she was back in her own bed, in her own room, on Christmas morning. Her head was full of memories of the night's magical events.

When she told her family about her wonderful adventure, they were sure it was only a dream. But Clara didn't mind. She felt sure that the nutcracker prince's battle with the Mouse King and her journey to the Kingdom of Sweets had really happened. And she never forgot them for as long as she lived.

Jingle Bells

Jingle bells, jingle bells,
Jingle all the way.
Oh, what fun it is to ride
In a one-horse open sleigh.
Jingle bells, jingle bells,
Jingle all the way.
Oh, what fun it is to ride
In a one-horse open sleigh.

A day or two ago,
I thought I'd take a ride,
And soon Miss Fannie Bright
Was seated by my side.
The horse was lean and lank,
Misfortune seemed his lot,
He got into a drifted bank,
And then we got upset.

Jingle bells, jingle bells,
Jingle all the way.
Oh, what fun it is to ride
In a one-horse open sleigh.
Jingle bells, jingle bells,
Jingle all the way.
Oh, what fun it is to ride
In a one-horse open sleigh.

Jingle Bells

Brightly

1. Dash-ing through the snow   In a   one-horse o-pen sleigh,

O'er the fields we go,   Laugh-ing all the way,   Bells on bob-tail ring,

Mak-ing spir-its bright. What   fun   it   is   to ride and sing A

sleigh-ing song to-night.   Jin-gle bells,   jin-gle bells,

Jin- gle all the way.   Oh, what fun it   is to ride In a

CHRISTMAS SUGAR COOKIES

Christmas cookies look festive — and taste delicious! Best of all, they're fun to make. But before you get started on a batch, be sure to ask a grown-up for help — especially with the baking.

WHAT YOU NEED

2/3 cup butter
or margarine

3/4 cup white sugar

1 egg

1/2 teaspoon
vanilla flavoring

2 cups all-purpose flour

2 teaspoons
baking powder

1/4 teaspoon salt

4 teaspoons milk

Cookie cutters in
Christmas shapes

How to make Christmas sugar cookies:

Again, make sure a grown-up is there to help you.

With an electric mixer, beat together the butter (or margarine) and sugar.

Then add the egg and vanilla extract.

Beat the mixture well and then set it aside.

In another bowl, sift together the flour, baking powder, and salt.

Mix the flour mixture with the first mixture a little at a time, while gradually adding milk.

Knead the cookie dough about a quarter at a time until it is blended smoothly.

Roll the dough on a lightly floured board until it is about 1/8 inch (2-3 millimeters) thick.

Cut the dough into different shapes. You can use cookie cutters for this, or you can simply cut out your own shapes with a knife. Be careful using the knife.

Place the shapes on a lightly greased cookie sheet. Bake in a preheated oven at 375 degrees Fahrenheit (191 degrees Celsius) for 10-12 minutes. Allow to cool before frosting.

FROSTING YOUR COOKIES

Use this simple frosting recipe to put the finishing touches on your cookies.
You can also add food coloring to the icing to create colored cookies.

WHAT YOU NEED

2 cups confectioners'
sugar

1/4 cup soft butter or
margarine

1 teaspoon vanilla
extract

Food coloring (optional)

Blend these ingredients together until they are smooth. If you want, you can add food coloring to make festive red or green frosting. If the mixture is too thick, try adding a few drops of milk. If the mixture is too thin, add a few more spoonfuls of sugar.

Here's an extra idea:

After the cookies are frosted, decorate them with chocolate sprinkles, colored sugar, or little silver sugar balls.

YUM!

CHRISTMAS ORNAMENTS
OF FLOUR CLAY

These fun-to-make ornaments look good enough to eat, but they're for decoration only. Paint them with poster paints and they'll stay bright for several Christmases to come!

WHAT YOU NEED

For the flour clay:

4 cups all-purpose flour

2 cups salt

1 teaspoon
baking powder

1 1/2 cups water

To decorate:

Poster paints

Clear shellac (optional)

Gold cord or wire,
glitter, sequins, etc.

Food coloring (optional)

Cookie cutters in
Christmas shapes

Fine sandpaper

A plastic straw

How to make Christmas flour ornaments:

**BE SURE TO ASK A
GROWN-UP TO HELP YOU.**

Mix all the ingredients together by hand in a bowl. If the dough seems too dry, try adding a teaspoon of water. You can also add food coloring to the dough if you want.

On a lightly floured surface, roll the dough out until it is about 1/8 inch (2-3 millimeters) thick. Cut out shapes with cookie cutters. You may also want to make your own shapes.

If you want to hang the ornaments, cut a hole in the top of each one, using the straw like a cookie cutter.

Now you're ready to start baking!

Remember to ask a grown-up to do this part.

Heat the oven to 250 degrees Fahrenheit (121 degrees Celsius). Put the ornaments on an ungreased baking sheet and bake for about 30 minutes. Remove them from oven and turn the ornaments over. Then bake them for about another hour, or until they are hard. Remove them from the baking sheet and allow them to cool.

Once the ornaments have cooled, you can decorate them with poster paints. Before you begin, smooth each ornament with fine sandpaper and draw whatever pattern you want on the ornament with a pencil. Then paint it. When the paint is dry, you can brush over the ornaments with clear shellac to protect the paint. Try sticking on sequins or gold glitter, too. Then string gold cord or wire through the holes, and your pretty ornaments will be ready for hanging!.

PAPER CANDY CANE ORNAMENTS

Candy canes have been a favorite Christmas tradition for years. Here are some colorful candy cane decorations you can make out of paper and hang on your tree!

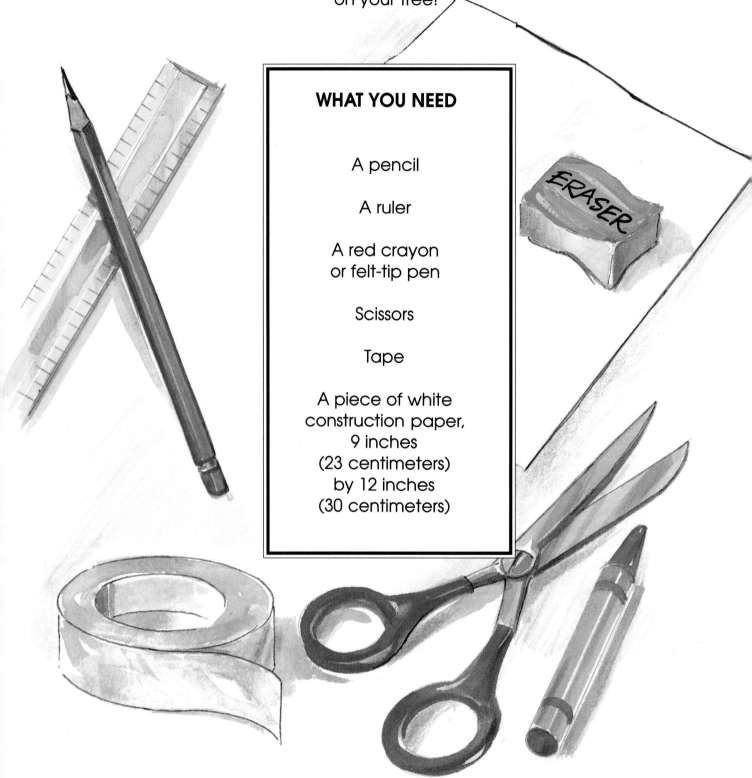

WHAT YOU NEED

A pencil

A ruler

A red crayon
or felt-tip pen

Scissors

Tape

A piece of white
construction paper,
9 inches
(23 centimeters)
by 12 inches
(30 centimeters)

How to make paper candy canes:

In pencil, mark out a square 9 inches (23 centimeters) by 9 inches (23 centimeters) on the piece of white construction paper.

Cut out the square.

Draw red lines on the square.

Turn the paper over and roll it up from the lower right corner (1) to the upper left corner (2).

Put a piece of tape over to secure it.

Trim the ends so that they are straight.

Bend one end over into a curl.

Now your pretty candy cane is ready to hang on your tree!

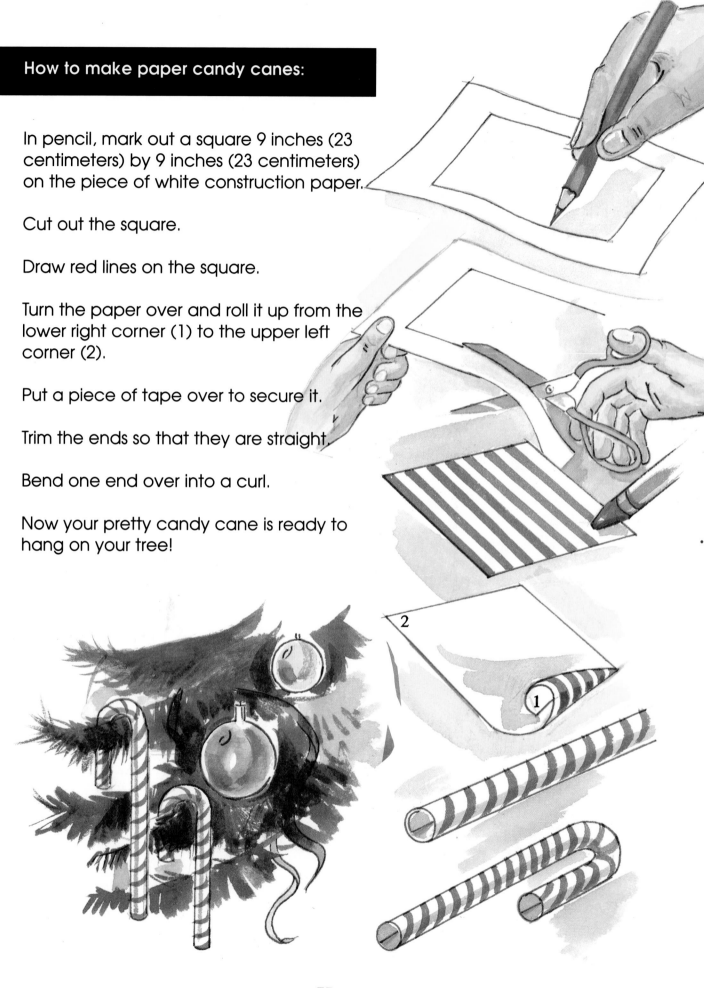

PAPER SNOWMAN CHAIN

You can make this paper snowman chain to hang on your Christmas tree.

WHAT YOU NEED

A sheet of white typing paper

A black, felt-tipped marker

Glue

Scissors

A pencil

A piece of string or colored yarn

GLUE

How to make your paper snowman chain:

Fold the sheet of paper in half lengthwise. Cut along the fold line and discard one half, or save it to make a second chain.

Fold the remaining sheet of paper in thirds crosswise. Then fold it in half.

Hold the folded paper and press firmly along the creases to keep it flat.

Now copy this snowman pattern onto the folded paper and carefully cut around the shape. Be sure not to cut through the folds at the arms and the sides of the body.

Open the paper out flat. With your felt-tipped marker, draw in two eyes, a nose, a mouth, and three buttons on each snowman (as below).

Glue a piece of string or colored yarn to the back of the first snowman and to the last snowman. Tie the strings to two different branches of your Christmas tree.

Or you can make a circle of snowmen. Glue the first and last snowmen together, putting a string in the seam so that you can hang it.

STAR TREE ORNAMENT

Here is a pretty ornament that is very easy to make and fun to decorate with gold glitter, sequins, or whatever you like.

WHAT YOU NEED

Thick construction paper or thin cardboard

A pencil

Tracing paper

A ruler

Scissors

White glue

Gold glitter and sequins (optional)

GLUE

TRACING PAPER

How to make the star:

Measure the construction paper or cardboard into 2 squares, each measuring 4 inches by 4 inches (10 centimeters by 10 centimeters), and cut the squares out.

Using tracing paper, trace the star shown on the right. When you have traced it, turn it over on one of the construction paper squares (with the pencil side down).

Draw carefully over the tracing paper star shape again. When you lift the tracing paper, the star shape will show up on the construction paper.

Now go over the tracing on the second construction paper square.

Cut the shapes out carefully.

Make a cut from the top point down to the middle of one star. Cut the other star from the bottom up to the center.

Turn one star around and slide the two stars together. Pull until the points meet at the top and the bottom.

To make your star sparkle, paint it with glue and sprinkle gold glitter on it. Hang your star by carefully making a hole in the top and threading gold cord through it. You can ask a grown-up to tie a knot to make a loop.

CHRISTMAS BUTTONS

You can give your friends a present that you have made yourself. Everyone will like these bright Christmas buttons. But don't forget to make one for yourself!

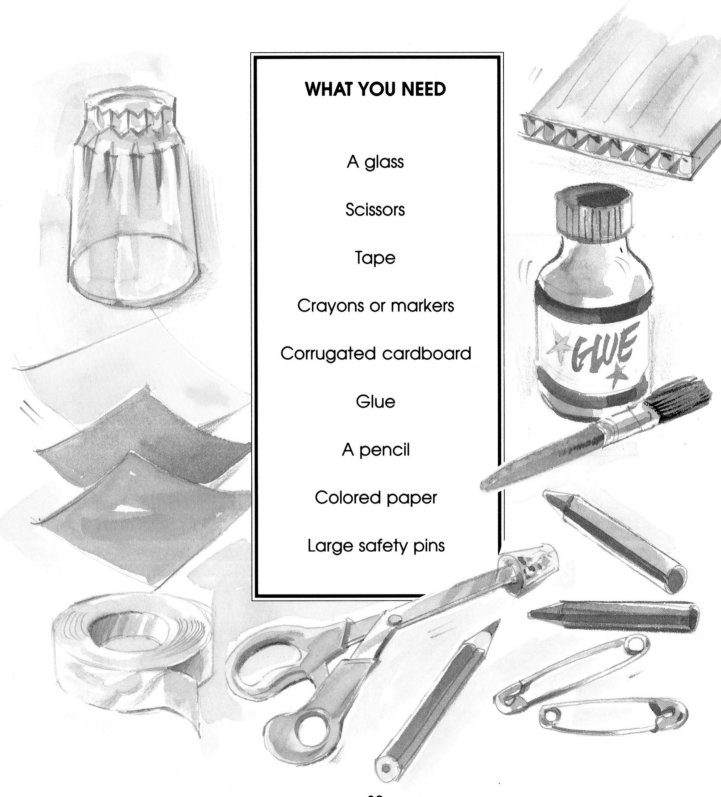

WHAT YOU NEED

A glass

Scissors

Tape

Crayons or markers

Corrugated cardboard

Glue

A pencil

Colored paper

Large safety pins

How to make a Christmas button:

Select a piece of colored paper for the background of each button. Place the rim of the glass on the paper and draw around the rim. This makes a circle. Cut out the circle you have drawn.

Glue the circle to the corrugated cardboard. Leave it to dry for a few minutes.

Draw Christmas designs on each button. You can use the ones shown here or design some of your own.

Cut out the button. Turn it over and tape a safety pin to the back of the button, as shown in the picture.

You can also add decorations to your button by cutting out pictures from old Christmas cards or magazines and gluing them onto your button.

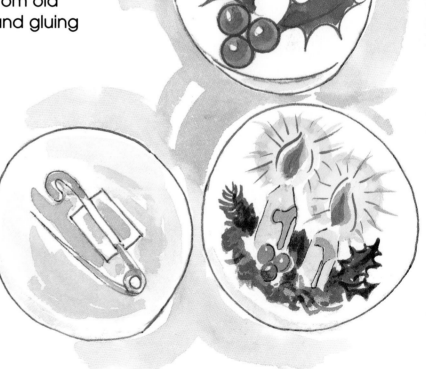

CARDBOARD ROLL
SANTA

Ho, ho, ho! Here's a jolly Santa Claus for you to make. What a merry decoration!

WHAT YOU NEED

Empty cardboard
bathroom tissue roll

Red construction
paper

White construction
paper

Black construction
paper

Cotton

Craft glue or tape

Crayons or colored
pencils

GLUE

How to make the cardboard roll Santa:

Wrap red construction paper around the roll, leaving about a half an inch (4 centimeters) uncovered. Glue or tape it securely.

Draw face with crayons or colored pencils. Be sure to give Santa rosy cheeks!

Wrap white construction paper around the rest, and glue or tape.

Cut out strips for arms (red), mittens and boots (black), and belt and buttons (black). Glue in place.

Cut out hat shape and assemble as shown. Glue in place on top of cardboard roll.

Now glue on lots of cotton for Santa's beard. Don't forget the fur trim around his hat and the pom-pom on the end!

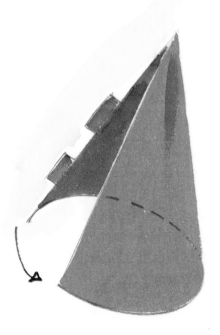

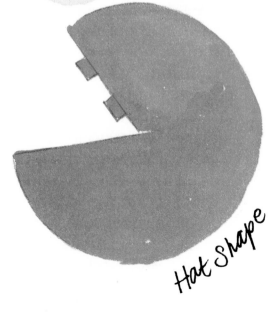

Hat Shape

The Elves and the Shoemaker

With Christmas fast approaching, the shoemaker wondered how he and his wife would survive. Times were very hard for them. And the day finally came when he had enough leather for only one more pair of shoes. It was a piece of beautiful red leather. Before he went to bed that night, the shoemaker cut it with extra care and laid it out on his bench to sew the next day. Then, he and his wife climbed the winding stairs to their bedroom, said their prayers, and fell asleep.

The following morning when he came downstairs, the shoemaker was amazed to find a pair of red shoes lying finished on his workbench. He examined them carefully. Never in his life had he seen a pair of shoes made more beautifully than these. Puzzled, he put the shoes on display in his shop window.

Later that day, a nobleman passing through the town called on the shoemaker. When he saw the red shoes, he immediately insisted on trying them on. They fit him perfectly, and he paid much more than the usual price for them.

Now the shoemaker had enough money to buy leather for two more pairs of shoes.

He cut the leather into pieces and laid them out on his workbench, as he had done before. Then he went to bed.

The next morning, two pairs of shoes lay on the workbench. They were beautifully sewn and polished, and were just waiting for a customer. Soon, these shoes had been sold, too.

Now the shoemaker had enough money to buy leather for four more pairs of shoes. Again, he found the shoes finished and waiting for him in the morning. And so it continued. Whatever the shoemaker cut out one day was always finished and waiting for him the next morning.

The shoemaker's fame began to spread. Customers came from far and wide. His shoes were declared to be the most comfortable, the most stylish, and the most beautifully made of any shoemaker's in the land. And far from being poor, he became rich.

One evening, his wife said to him, "Let's stay up tonight and see who is bringing us such good fortune."

The shoemaker's wife lit a candle and placed it near the work-bench. Then she and her husband crouched in a dark corner of the shop. There, they waited.

Around midnight, two tiny elves came into the room. They immediately took up the leather and hammered and stitched it with their tiny fingers. In no time, they had finished one pair of shoes. The shoemaker could hardly believe his eyes. They immediately started on another pair and never stopped working until they had finished all the work that was lying on the bench. Then they ran away.

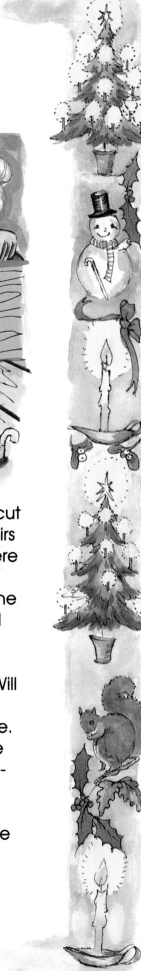

The shoemaker and his wife came out of their dark corner. His wife said, "These little elves have changed our lives. We must thank them. I will make them some clothes, and you shall make each of them a new pair of shoes."

The shoemaker gladly agreed, and all that day he and his wife cut and stitched. By evening, two little shirts, two pairs of trousers, two pairs of socks, two red knitted hats, and two pairs of fine pointed shoes were ready.

Again, the shoemaker and his wife hid themselves. And again, the tiny elves appeared. When they saw the lovely clothes, they hugged each other in delight. They tried them on, and hopped and danced around the room with glee. Then they ran off.

The shoemaker and his wife looked at each other and asked, "Will they come again tomorrow night?" But the elves never came back.

Still, it was a very happy Christmas for the shoemaker and his wife. He became more and more famous. Soon, he made shoes for all the lords and ladies in the land. Even the king, when he wanted an extra-special pair of shoes, would send for the shoemaker and ask him to make them.

And so, thanks to the little elves, the shoemaker and his wife were never poor again. They had good luck the rest of their lives.

Jolly Old Saint Nicholas

2. When the clock is striking twelve,
When I'm fast asleep,
Down the chimney broad and black,
With your pack you'll creep.
All the stockings you will find
Hanging in a row.
Mine will be the shortest one,
You'll be sure to know.

3. Susie wants a pair of skates,
Johnny wants a train,
Kelly wants a baseball glove,
Billy wants a game.
As for me, I can't decide,
What I'd like that night.
Choose for me, old Santa Claus,
What you think is right.

Here We Come A-Caroling

2. We are not daily beggars
That beg from door to door.
But we are neighbors' children
Whom you have seen before.
Chorus
Love and Joy come to you,
And to you your carol too,
And God bless you and send you
A happy New Year,
And God send you a happy New Year.

3. Call up the butler of this house,
Put on his golden ring.
Let him bring us a glass of milk,
And the better we shall sing.
Chorus
Love and joy come to you,
And to you your carol too,
And God bless you and send you
A happy New Year,
And God send you a happy New Year.

4. God bless the master of this house,
Likewise the mistress, too.
And all the little children
That round the table go.
Chorus
Love and Joy come to you,
And to you your carol too,
And God bless you and send you
A happy New Year,
And God send you a happy New Year.

Good King Wenceslas

2. "Hither, page, and stand by me,
If thou know'st it, telling,
Yonder peasant who is he?
Where and what his dwelling?"
"Sire, he lives a good league hence,
Underneath the mountain,
Right against the forest fence
By Saint Agnes' fountain."

3. "Bring me flesh and bring me wine.
Bring me pine logs hither.
Thou and I will see him dine,
When we bear them thither."
Page and monarch, forth they went,
Forth they went together,
Through the rude wind's wild lament
And the bitter weather.

4. "Sire, the night is darker now,
And the wind blows stronger.
Fails my heart, I know not how;
I can go no longer."
"Mark my footsteps good, my page;
Tread thou in them boldly.
Thou shalt find the winter's rage
Freeze thy blood less coldly."

5. In his master's steps he trod,
Where the snow lay dinted;
Heat was in the very sod,
Which the saint had printed.
Therefore, Christian men, be sure,
Wealth or rank possessing,
Ye who now will bless the poor
Shall yourselves find blessing.

We Wish You a Merry Christmas

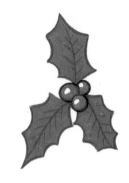

We Wish You a Merry Christmas

2. Now bring us some figgy pudding,
Now bring us some figgy pudding,
Now bring us some figgy pudding
And bring some out here.

Good tidings we bring
To you and your kin;
We wish you a merry Christmas,
And a happy New Year.

3. For we all like figgy pudding,
For we all like figgy pudding,
For we all like figgy pudding
So bring some out here.

Good tidings we bring
To you and your kin;
We wish you a merry Christmas,
And a happy New Year.

And we won't go until we've got some,
And we won't go until we've got some,
And we won't go until we've got some
So bring some out here.

Good tidings we bring
To you and your kin;
We wish you a merry Christmas,
And a happy New Year.